Birds of Prey!

Written by Bendix Anderson
Illustrated by Mike Maydak

**Reviewed by John Rowden, Ph.D., Bird Department,
Wildlife Conservation Society/Bronx Zoo, New York.**

© 2000 McClanahan Book Company, Inc.
All rights reserved.
Published by McClanahan Book Company, Inc.
A Division of Learning Horizons
1 American Road, Cleveland OH 44144
ISBN: 0-7681-0232-4
Printed in the U.S.A.
10 9 8 7 6 5 4 3 2 1

What's that in the sky?

Can you see it? It's too small to be an airplane. It's too big to be a robin or a sparrow. It's moving very fast, and it's coming closer. It's a . . .

Quick!

Turn the page to find out . . .

Bird of prey!

To **prey** means to hunt—so birds of prey are birds that hunt other animals to survive. They eat small mammals, fish, snakes and lizards, insects, and even other birds!

Bald Eagle

Owls, hawks, falcons, and eagles are birds of prey. Vultures are also birds of prey even though they hunt differently from their cousins.

How they Hunt

These birds can spot their prey from far away. Then they attack with their sharp claws, called **talons** (TAL-luns). They have four talons on each foot to snatch up their dinner. They eat with their curved, pointed beaks.

Redtailed Hawk

A Harpy Eagle's talons can be up to 10 inches (12 cm) long.

Redtailed Hawk

Night Birds

Owls are the only birds of prey that are **nocturnal** (KNOCK-turn-all)—they are active mostly at night. They have good hearing and eyesight to help them hunt in the dark. Owls can hear tiny mice walking in tall grass and see bats flying against the night sky.

Barn Owl

Sharp-eyed Hawks

Hawks have keen eyesight for spotting prey in the daytime. They also have powerful wings that help them fly high, change direction quickly, and dive.

Sharp-shinned Hawk

Many hawks travel thousands of miles between their summer and winter homes. This is called **migration** (my-GRAY-shun).

Little Hawks, Big Hawks

Red-shouldered Hawk
40 inches (102 cm)

Ferruginous Hawk
54 inches (137 cm)

Sharp-shinned Hawk
28 inches (71 cm)

High-flying Falcons

Falcons can fly higher than the tallest buildings. When a falcon sees something it wants to catch, it folds its wings back and dives at great speed. As it nears its prey, the falcon spreads its wings and thrusts its talons forward to grab its dinner. Peregrine falcons can catch pigeons in midair!

Baby Peregrine Falcons nesting on a rooftop

Peregrine Falcon

Awesome Eagles

Eagles are the strongest birds of prey. They are in the same family as hawks, but eagles can generally fly higher, dive faster, and hunt larger prey.

An eagle will sometimes steal another bird's food!

Golden Eagle

Most eagles hunt for birds and mammals. But some eagles, including the American bald eagle, eat fish. Bateleur eagles in Africa sometimes eat poisonous snakes! They have thick scaly skin on their legs that snakes cannot bite through.

Bateleur Eagle

Big and Bigger

Little Eagle
4 feet (1.2 m)

Bonelli's Eagle
5.5 feet (1.7 m)

Bald Eagle
7 feet (2.1 m)

Voracious Vultures

Most birds of prey hunt living creatures, but vultures hunt for meat that is already dead! This dead meat is called **carrion** (CARE-ee-on).

Vultures may fly 100 miles (160 km) or more in search of a meal.

Turkey Vultures

When other hunters leave the remains of a meal, or when an animal dies of old age, vultures find the body and eat it. This may seem really gross, but vultures are performing an important clean-up job—they're like the garbage men of nature.

Wide Wings

Turkey Vulture
6 feet (2 m)

Andean Condor
10 feet (3 m)

Bird Houses

Most birds of prey mate for life. Like many other birds, they may make a nest. Eagles return to the same nest every year and keep adding on sticks, leaves, pine needles, grass, and even moss. Bald eagle nests may end up being 20 feet (6 m) tall!

Peregrine Falcons

The high nest of a bird of prey is called an **aerie** (air-EE).

Bald Eagle chicks

Burrowing Owl

Turkey Vulture

Some birds of prey don't use sticks in their nests. A crevice in a rocky cliff is enough for them. Some vultures and owls nest in hollow trees. Burrowing Owls live underground in places such as abandoned gopher holes!

Baby Birds of Prey

All birds of prey lay eggs. The parents take turns sitting on the eggs to keep them warm. When the eggs finally hatch, the baby birds are very small and weak. The parents must protect the chicks from animals such as raccoons, snakes, and even other birds of prey!

The parents bring their chicks meat to eat so they can grow strong. As soon as they are able to fly, the young birds leave the nest. But they may stay close to their parents for a while to get extra food and to learn how to hunt.

Young Golden Eagles

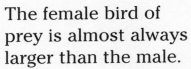

Bet you didn't know...

The female bird of prey is almost always larger than the male.

female

male

Owls have very flexible necks. They can literally look over their shoulder!

The American 25-cent piece
has a bird of prey on one side.
Can you tell which bird it is?

In 1973, a Rupell's vulture hit
an airplane flying 37,000 feet
(11,200 m) over Africa!

On a clear day, a peregrine
falcon can see a pigeon
5 miles (8 km) away!

So if you see a bird of prey, just think . . .

Bald Eagle

it probably saw you first!